Beginner's Guide to Free-Motion Quilting

Table of Contents

Introduction

In this guide, we will look at all the necessary aspects, from the basics. You will find in-depth information on the tools you need, how to prepare your machine, choice of needles and threads, the use of stencils and markings, basting, adjusting tension, and preparing your own designs. You will only need to make practice a consistent companion.

Some people may find free-motion quilting a bit challenging, especially because you may not achieve the even and perfectly spaced stitches that come with the craft. Besides, things can also get ugly! You can have a mix of small and big stitches spaced as if they had an attitude of their own. In essence, free-motion quilting hands you the power to create as you go, make patterns, give life and beauty to the quilt, and ultimately own it. There is just one rule—there are no boundaries, the sky's the limit, and this is a hobby that is supposed to make you happy.

Take up the challenge and let us subdue free-motion quilting. Aside from fun, and the everyday purpose of quilts, do you know you can pass secret messages, express your mood, and show your feelings through them? African-American slaves used quilts hung in the open to pass messages. The quilts even included directions and maps. You see how much you can pour out into a quilt?

Let's get right into it and fill our days with joy, control, beautiful quilts, and a sense of achievement!

Chapter 1:
Features of a Free-Motion Quilting Machine

Today, there is a wide variety of machines to choose from. Let us look at the key features you need to look for, irrespective of the size of your budget. You want a machine that makes quilting fun and smooth and not a frustrating affair. A machine that caters to the unique concepts of free-motion quilting.

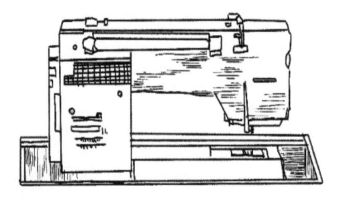

The basic requirements include:

- **Working space**—Space is crucial when doing free-motion quilting because you have to move the quilt easily. Therefore, it is necessary that your machine has a big throat. The machine's throat is the area behind the needle that it encloses, also referred to as the harp. A big throat ensures that you can easily handle the material without having to reroll, reposition, or fold the quilt, since you have space to stuff the material.

A long arm, again the machine's and not yours, is ideal for free-motion quilting. The arm refers to the distance between the needle and the machine's vertical part. A long machine arm allows for an easier creation of larger patterns. You can manoeuvre the fabric without much resistance. You are better off with a machine with a long arm and big throat for optimal working space.

- **Feed dog**—The term does not refer to a dog's dinner. In a sewing machine, feed dogs are metal-like ridges that begin from a hole on the throat and usually move as you sew. They grip the bottom fabric, helping it to pass through the machine and produce a stitch of high-quality. In most cases, sewing happens with feed dogs facing upwards and visible, but in the case of free-motion quilting, the feed dogs are lowered or covered.

Lowering the feed dogs means that the machine does not grip the fabric's underside, giving you full control of the length and position of the stitches. In free-motion quilting, that is the ideal situation. Your choice of a machine must make it easy to move the feed.

Most machines have a switch to lower the feed dogs, although older versions may have a cover. If your machine does not lower the feed dog, you can improvise by using playing cards or a piece of plastic as a cover. Whatever the feature of your machine, you need to have enough room to move the fabric around without the feed dog inhibiting your movement.

- **Presser foot pressure dial**—As a free-motion quilter, it is best to use a darning foot. They may differ depending on the machine, but generally, they have a base with a circular opening. A darning foot allows you to manoeuvre the fabric with ease and in any direction. With the clear sole, you have maximum visibility to quilt away happily.

The foot pressure adjustment dial is important in setting the amount of pressure placed on the fabric by the pressure foot. Different fabrics require different amounts of pressure.

Nowadays, there are computerised stitch regulators that, once set, can produce consistent lengths of stitches during free-motion quilting, even with lowered feed dogs.

- **Knee lifter**—You will need a knee lifter to raise and lower your presser foot without using your hands. Your machine of choice should allow you to use your knee to raise and lower the presser foot. In free-motion quilting, you are the one in charge, and the hands play a crucial role in moving the fabric. You need those hands free and dedicated to the task at hand. Sometimes, it is not a knee press, but rather it might be implanted in your machine in the form of a button or heel press. If it's in a flywheel, it might be a bit bulky but it's doable.

- **Needle stop down function**—You need your needle to stop in your fabric every time you let the foot feed up. The needle stop down function helps the quilt from moving and shifting each time you stop sewing because the needle being down and in the fabric holds and prevents it from moving. You can then adjust your fabric or position it well without losing the pattern. As you choose a machine, this is an important feature to look for.

- **Half stitch**—This capability is important. You have to bring up a bobbin thread, which you will learn further along in this book.

Accessories

Now that you know the best features to look for in a free-motion quilting machine, you may want to know the extras. We all love something extra, and if you need evidence walk into a store and watch the items that come with something *extra* fly off the shelf. Even in quilting, it is always nice to have something that makes life more cheerful or eases things.

Although your machine has all the necessary features, there are a few items that you can add to make your quilting journey smooth and pleasant. You don't have to get them, but it would be beneficial to have them.

- **A free-motion quilting foot**—If you can only have one accessory, then have this one. A free-motion quilting foot does not impair your vision. You, therefore, can move the quilt freely and see your work clearly. There will be no guessing how the stitch looks or pulling it out to see. The good news is that you have choices; you can choose stable or hopping, metal or clear, closed or open. You may need to consult your machine's manual to find the right type.

However, there are generic feet available on the market, and you can always opt for one of those if you are unsatisfied.

- **Extension table**—You want to work as comfortably as possible, and an extension table will do just that for you. The extension is a rectangular platform made of plastic that is designed to fit around your quilting machine securely. Its work is to extend your working surface to the height of the needle. You can therefore, easily support your quilt and free-motion quilt for longer without hand fatigue. Additionally, you can create nice shapes and designs because the quilt does not drag off the edge and can move smoothly. You may be excited to get this one, especially because of how it will allow you to work longer. However, before you do, you may want to ensure a correct fit. Your best bet is to find one made by your machine's manufacturer. Alternatively, you can look for a universal sewing table.

- **Walking foot**—Most quilters will own this piece of equipment, which is larger than the typical presser foot, and although more costly, it is worth the extra money. There is no assurance that your machine will come with one, so you may want to buy. The walking foot helps stitch all the layers together without any of them shifting.

- **Supreme slider**—You want your quilting to be smooth, and this slick sheet of plastic that clings to the bed of the sewing machine will come in handy. The plastic sheet creates a smooth surface covering for the machine's feed dogs, with a small rectangle cut left for the needle hole. If you have a domestic machine for free-motion quilting, then the supreme slider was created for you. It also peels off and on easily. The extra slick surface helps to move the quilt under the needle effortlessly, reduce fatigue, and spring some joy into free-motion quilting.

- **Quilting guide**—If you have a hard time keeping the surface of your quilt flat during free-motion quilting, then a quilting guide may be what you need. The guide is a weighted ring with a covering of a rubbery surface whose job is to grip the quilt. All you have to do is place it on the quilt, then work within the ring. Since the quilt is held flat by the ring, you will have a clear view of your work and only have to move the ring and not the quilt.

Chapter Summary

Your free-motion quilting machine needs to have various key features, such as an adequate working space, knee lifter, ability to lower the feed dogs, darning foot, and needle down function. You can add some accessories like a free-motion quilting foot, extension table, quilting guide, or supreme slider.

In the next chapter, you will learn about needles and threads, including how to choose the appropriate one for each project.

Chapter 2:
Needles and Thread

The next step is to choose your needles and threads. You can be forgiven for thinking that these are not as important. The truth is that a thread is not just a thread, and neither is a needle universal. If you are to enjoy free-motion quilting, then you must know your needles and thread and use the appropriate one each time.

Thread

Looking at a quilt and its defined patterns, one thing that stands out is the thread because it is what brings out the pattern. Although most people may take the thread for granted, it plays a decorative role, in addition to binding the layers of the quilt together. In a way, the thread can help make or break your quilting job.

Many beginners think that cotton thread is the best and continually use it because of its pure form in terms of color and hue. However, the market today has a wide variety and you can choose what goes best with your fabric. When starting, you can use a lightweight, fine thread for free-motion quilting like thin cotton. A cotton thread of 50 weight is ideal, as it has enough strength to keep it from breaking and easily keeps the right tension to give even stitches. Using a thin cotton thread in both the top and bobbin balances the tension. However, you can vary the thread by using different weights.

Weight of the Thread

You will come across a reference to the weight of the thread in this guide. Do not bother buying a scale for that purpose. The weight of the thread, usually abbreviated as "wt," simply refers to its thinness and fineness. The higher the number, the finer it is. If you find yourself thinking it should be the opposite, you are not alone. To be clear, a thread weight of 80 means a thinner thread, whereas 30wt is much thicker.

Thread Tex

Tex refers to the density of the thread's fibers, usually measured in grams per 1000 meters. When the tex is larger, the thread is heavier. Note that tex is more common in Canada and Europe.

Denier

Denier, also abbreviated as "d," is the unit of yarn fineness that is equivalent to the fineness of one gram for every 9000 meters. Therefore, a 150-denier yarn is not as fine as a 100-denier yarn. The higher the denier, the thicker the thread. Note that not all countries use Denier.

Thread Material

As mentioned earlier, thread no longer comes in cotton only. Today, there is an entire world of threads out there, all waiting for you to discover and behold their different personalities. Yes, they do come with different attitudes. Some are temperamental and will snap at any extra pull,some are strong and will take in more tension, and yet others are beautiful and take the center stage. There are even combinations that offer a mix of characters. Let us look at some of the most common thread materials used in free-motion quilting.

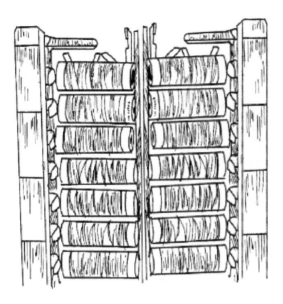

Common Thread Materials

Cotton—Cotton threads are some of the most commonly used. The cotton plant is spun to produce a cotton thread that is ideal for not only quilting, but also other sewing projects. Cotton thread is both resilient and versatile.

Nylon—Nylon thread is renowned for its strength, but it cannot withstand the heat. Being a synthetic elastic, the nylon thread melts at high temperatures.

Linen—The thread originates from the linen plant, and in most cases, it is spun heavy. You may find some that are coated in wax, which helps improve its durability.

Polyester—Polyester is synthetic, though it still does not match the strength of nylon. On the other hand, it is much stronger than cotton and can boast much flexibility and resilience to the many issues that affect the relationship between the fabric and thread-like melting, linting, and shrinking.

Cotton/Polyester blend—This is one of the more popular thread materials, widely used by quilters. The combination of cotton and polyester has the best of both worlds; polyester's strength and flexibility, along with cotton's appearance.

Silk—You may have learned about how silk is fine, and that is true. Silk thread is fine, but do not mistake its look for weakness. Packed in its fine strands is strength. Silkworms are the ones tasked with providing us with this high-sheen thread that radiates class. Most people use it for detailing because of its thinness.

Rayon—Like polyester and nylon, rayon is synthetic and mainly used in embroidery. What lets this thread down is its vulnerability to color fading, either from washing or over time.

Wool—Nearly everyone knows about wool and its heaviness. We tend to associate wool with warmth and not smoothness.

Types of Thread

You may have heard of metallic thread and wondered how it fits into a metallic needle. You most likely heard of a few types of thread-like bobbins and embroidery. The world of threads is deep, and in this guide, we will only scratch the surface looking at some of the common ones used in quilting. Since this is the beginning, feel free to keep delving deeper and trying out different types.

Bobbin—The bobbin thread is thin. It is embroidery that comes pre-wound and sold in large quantities that are spun on cones or in regular spools. All you have to do is pop on your machine if it uses bobbin.

All-purpose—If you have no idea what thread to use or are unsure, then the all-purpose has your back. Usually cotton—or a blend of cotton, the all-purpose is suitable for most free-motion quilting projects not unless you want a particularly thicker or thinner thread.

Metallic or Decorative—If you are looking for a thread with a bit of shine, then this is the thread for you. Nowadays, the metallic thread has gained popularity for its ability to throw the dull out of the window. The thread is called metallic because it has a coating of a thin layer of metallic texture, glitter, or color on the thread strands. At times, the thread may have all: color, texture, and glitter.

Water-soluble—Some threads disintegrate in water and are mainly temporary. You want to use such a thread during the basting of quilts or hold pieces together for a while. With this thread, after the purpose is done, you do not need to pick out the stitches you put in water, since they will have disappeared! Of course, this is not desirable for free-motion quilting. Here, stitches matter; in fact, they have a strong voice and make decisions on how the final project will turn out.

Quilting—You cannot use water-soluble thread, but you can use quilting thread, which is typically made of polyester, cotton, or a blend of both. The good news is that quilting thread is ideal for both hand and machine quilting. Don't relax too much though; although it may work for most projects and people, some may need to find something more specific.

Fusible—Mainly used in binding and applique, fusible thread, as the name implies, fuses anything that is in contact with it when heated. Some people use an iron to make the fuse. If you do not intend to make a fuse, you should avoid ironing this type of thread.

Embroidery—The choice is wide; it could be made of polyester, silk, rayon, or cotton. You can tell from its name that it specializes in embroidering, either by machine or hand. Embroidery threads come in small skeins and a myriad of colors.

Choice of Thread

With threads, you have to be open to experimenting. The same combination of threads may work beautifully on one piece, but border on the disaster on another. You should be willing to experiment beforehand, looking at the outcome of different threads on the type of fabric you intend to use for your project before deciding what is best. Once you have made your choice, you can then begin working on your quilt.

To start you off, here are some tips that can help you choose the appropriate thread:

- If you are looking for a star-of-the-party kind of quilt—one that is noticeable, attractive, and not easy to ignore—then you need to choose a thread of a heavier weight. 30, 40, or 50 is ideal.

- For your thread to blend well with the top of your quilt and have a great overall texture, it is best to make your thread finer, like 80 or 100.

- Choose a color that contrasts with your quilt top to make your project pop.

- Know your machine intimately, if possible. Some machines do well with certain threads. For example, the bobbin thread is suitable for machines with bobbins. Manufacturers make some threads specifically for certain machines.

- Read your machine's guidelines and instructions well, so you can tell if it allows for thread with either medium or heavy weight.

Needles

For many of us, we may use the same sewing kit for years. Why fix what is broken? Many quilters face the same dilemma. Some start each project with a new sharp needle, whereas some use theirs until it does not work anymore—either blunt or broken.

Many beginners get confused by the wide range of needles available on the market today. If you are one of them, you are not alone. Many quilters find needle selection to be a daunting task, with many of them opting to use whatever is in the sewing machine. There are simple guidelines you can follow to ease the process and ensure that the needle makes the quilting process enjoyable and effective.

1. **The choice of a needle depends on the weight of the preferred thread**—The two work jointly, and hence should be a match. As a guideline, a 40 weight thread pairs well with a needle of size 75. If you choose a heavier thread, you should increase your needle size. The lighter your thread, the smaller your needle.

2. **Choose a needle by type of fabric and type of thread**—For example, a metallic thread goes with the metallic needle. It has a

special layer of Teflon, which cuts down any generated heat. Choosing a needle based on the type of thread or fabric can get complicated. The needle may work for the thread and not the fabric, or vice versa. When choosing a needle in such a scenario, you can consider the following:

- **Type of thread**—When using a specialty thread, you should opt for an embroidery needle or topstitch because their eyes are large. Choose your thread first, then look at compatible options.

- **Type of needlepoint**—Is a sharp needlepoint ideal or one that is slightly rounded? A sharp needlepoint penetrates fabrics that have a high thread count like batik or those with coated designs. However, the penetration leaves the fabric with micro-tears. Topstitch and microtex are some examples of sharp needles.

Using a slightly rounded needle point will allow for stitching between the fibers of the thread without damaging the fiber. If this is a better fit for your free-motion quilting project, then you could choose a quilting, embroidery, or universal needle. If you belong to a group that is not very enthusiastic about changing the machine needle, then rounded needles can offer you some great results.

Your choice of needle will depend on the fabric. As we have seen, you cannot use a rounded needlepoint for fabrics like batik. Once you have determined the type to use, you can choose the size to use, as per your thread.

If you are working with a tight budget, then a universal needle may be best. However, remember to keep the success of the entire project in mind and do not compromise for a few pennies. After all, the needle tends to be the cheapest part of any free-motion quilting exercise.

Again, there are no specific needles; you should always choose what to work with depending on the project. Different machines and fabrics should all influence your decision for needle type. You should always be open to experimentation.

As a rule of thumb, always have an extra sandwich of a quilt with you to try out your combination of needles and threads. You may want to keep noting down what you tried for each to avoid a situation where you find the match but cannot remember which needles or threads you used. Ensure that material used in this dummy quilt is the same one you intend to use for your project.

Chapter Summary

You need to keep in mind that:

- There are different kinds of thread, so take time to learn and explore them all.

- Your choice of thread will depend on the fabric you are working with; a heavier fabric needs a thicker thread.

- Understand your machine well; that way, you can choose the right thread for it.

- Your needle choice will also depend on the fabric and thread you are using. Ensure that your thread can easily fit in the needle, but not too loose that it keeps falling off.

Chapter 3:
Stitching in a Ditch

Stitching in a ditch is a very tricky exercise and requires much constant practice. Still, you can learn how to master the process. In this chapter, I will teach you how to quilt on a ditch and doodle some designs to enhance its aesthetics. I will also take you through some doodle designs to up your stitching skills a bit. But before that, digest this simple guide on how to quilt on a ditch.

Required Materials

- A ditch to quilt on.

- Threads (dark color, or those that match your fabric).

- Needle (based on your threads).

- Gloves (if necessary).

- A pair of scissors.

- Walking foot.

Instructions

Step 1. Ready the ditch for quilting.

Step 2. Needle and thread the quilting machine.

Step 3. Change machine foot from default to walking foot; its feeding dog will help you quilt in a straight line.

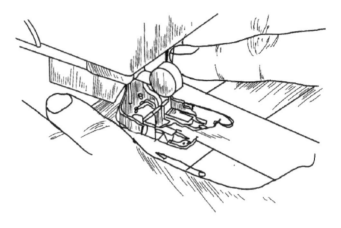

Step 4. Arrange your ditch sandwich carefully to fix the first seam on the walking foot.

Step 5. Quilt from one part to the other, but in a straight line.

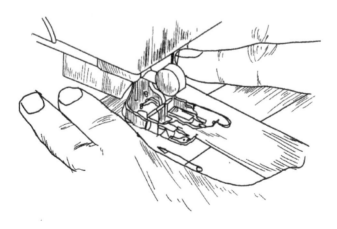

Step 6. Lift the walking foot, rotate the quilt counter clockwise, align the next seam accordingly, and lower the walking foot to jump stitch to another seam. Repeat the process until you finished quilting all the seams.

Step 7. Switch the foot back to free-motion mode, then quilt the sections within the blocks.

Step 8. Quilt seams in small sections of the blocks first. Then, doodle a few wavy-type designs in the ditches.

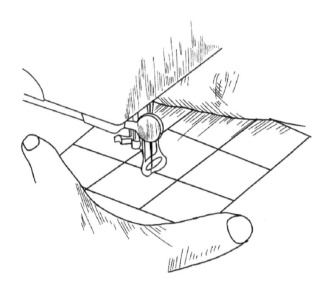

Step 9. Cut hanging threads off the jump stitches.

Congratulations! You have just finished quilting on a ditch. Next, we will discuss how you can stitch in the quilt.

How to Stitch in a Ditch Quilting

Placing stitches in a seam or close to it is difficult for some quilters, but it is something you can easily master. First, design your stitch outline, which could be ¼" or ⅛" away from your seam lines. So, whether you are working on a matching or a monofilament thread, you will always need to consider your stitch outline. Again, do away with thick threads that resemble a fishing line because they can mess up the whole show. Here is how you can run the stitch in a ditch quilting process.

Required Materials

- Two different fabrics.

- Sewing machine.

Instructions

Step 1. Examine the Quilt—Take your time examining the quilt and decide how you will press the seam allowances.

Step 2. Drop the Needle—Place the two fabrics on the seam and drop the sewing machine's needle on them, even as the bobbin thread hits the quilt.

Step 3. Place the Needle—Check the higher side of the seam to see where the allowance is pressed, but feel free to adjust the stitches by lowering the other side of the line. Tilt your needle down a bit to attain the best placement.

Step 4. Stitch on a Straight Line—Pull your fabrics apart a bit on both sides while you stitch in a straight line. Join the quilt to the end of the seam. Don't panic if your seams are inconsistent; it happens. Maintain a smooth stitch and keep the line straight.

Step 5. Add Quilting Motifs—You can add additional quilting motifs at this point, especially if your quilt has large patches. Should you need to add quilting motifs, read the instructions on your quilt batting before sewing them.

How to Make Bias Tape

Bias tape is an advanced and time-consuming stitch in a ditch design. Still, it is one design you'll love to do because you can tailor it to match the color of your fabric. Again, the bias tape is cost-friendly. Here, I will teach you how to create a unique bias tape through the piercing method.

Required Materials

- A piece of fabric.

- Half-inch clover bias tape maker.

Instructions

Step 1. Cut Your Fabric into Rectangular Tapes—Multiply the length of your fabric by its width. Divide the result by the width of the strips you need to get the estimated number of possible tapes from the fabric.

Step 2. Form the Bias—Gently fold the fabric to align the edges and form a triangle. Press the fold a bit to show a pressed line, also known as bias grain.

Step 3. Mark off Strip Lines—Ensure the width of your strips doubles that of the bias tape. The width will be shortened around the corner of the bias.

Step 4. Cut out the Strips and tug the strips a bit to stretch them.

Step 5. Trim the edges of the strips to flatten them.

Step 6. Join the right sides of two strips and sew them diagonally. Sew other small strips carefully and gradually until you have a long strip, but make sure everything turns to the same direction.

Step 7. Trim the edges of seam allowances and open them.

Step 8. Press the metal bar on the bias tape marker gently to feed the strip evenly.

Here is your single-fold bias. Feel free to fold it in half to make it a double-fold bias.

How to Make Bind Quilts

There is quilting, and then there is binding Follow these simple steps to bind your quilts.

Step 1. Cut Your Binding Strips—Add the width and length of your quilt and multiply the result by 2 to figure out the perimeter of your quilt. Add 10 inches, which would accommodate corners and seams. For example, here is how you would calculate your binding if your quilt was 52 by 70 inches:

$$52'' + 52'' + 70'' + 70'' + 10'' = 254''$$

So, you will need 254 inches of fabric to cut your binding strips. Next, divide the measurement by 40 to get the exact number of strips to cut. Result here is

6.35", so cut 7 strips of fabric. Again, decide on the size of binding you want to make. Cut your strips 2¼" wide if you want the front and back to be ¼".

Step 2. Sew the Binding across its Length— Join two right strips at a 90-degree angle, but sew them diagonally at a 45-degree angle. Feel free to draw a diagonal straight line from one end to another to aid the sewing exercise. However, if your fabric is solid, you'll have to pin or tape the right part of the fabric to avoid sewing the wrong side.

Step 3. Press the left side of the binding thoroughly to the end of its length.

Step 4. Join the Binding to the Quilt— Square off excess backing and batting from the quilt before you attach the binding. Although a large square ruler can be used to clean up the corners, a long, straight ruler will be fine for the sides. Run the binding along the edges of your quilt to prevent the seams from falling to the corners.

Step 5. Secure the Binding with Clips before you hand-stitch them.

Step 6. Hand-Stitch the Binding—Thread some needles to hand-stitch the binding and create a quilter's pattern. You can double the thread if you want the binding to last longer.

So, you now know to bind a quilt. You should work on several borders and corners to make more amazing and unique binds, as well.

How to Make a Waistband

Designing a waistband is no big deal once you understand the method we used to make the bias tape earlier. A waistband is very easy to make, and you can do it right there in your home. Just follow the steps here to design your own, home-made waistband.

Step 1. Stitch the Waistband—Carefully consider the seam allowance in the waistband pattern before you stitch the fabric. You will still need to join the right sides of the waistband to your skirt once you're set to run the stitching process.

Step 2. Press the Wrong (Left) Side to Make the Waistband Flat—Again, tilt the seam allowance on the waistband and press it between ¼ and ½ inches.

Step 3. Fold and Press the Waistband on the Wrong Side until the stitching line is covered fully. Pin the waistband until you start the stitching process.

Step 4. Stitch the Seam to the Skirt, but let it overlap a bit at the back. You can use your presser foot to stitch the seam to your skirts.

You can sew the seams with a decorative stitch if you want your stitching to be partially visible.

String Quilts

Use the string piercing method to make your string quilts. String piercing, being a free-form quilting style, does not require you to mark out a pattern. You only need to position your strips, sew the seam allowance, flip up the right side of the strip, and add another strip until you have designed your favorite string quilt. String quilt derived its name from strings—the fabric used to design it. You can definitely use your favorite fabric, but ensure the fabric is thick enough to conceal the string blocks. Should you want to sew strings on a printed fabric, flip the fabric to its wrong side. Remember that the right side houses the print.

String Quilting Tricks

- Use a variety of strips of fabric for strings, not just straight strips. Cut both straight and angled edge strips.

- Care less about fabric grain placement, since the strips will stabilize the strings.

- Don't color match. Combine several colors and fabric styles to make your string quilt charming.

- Opt for quilting fabrics with several color values.

- Vary the widths of your strings. Strips for an 8" block or more should be between 1¼" and 2½" wide, whereas smaller blocks or miniatures should have narrower widths.

- Muslin and other pre-washed cotton fabric could be used as a foundation for the string quilt block.

- Consider beige or gray threads because they look great on every fabric, but feel free to use any thread you want.

How to Make a String Quilt

Step 1. Cut your fabric to a 9"×9" square.

Step 2. Position the fabric diagonally, right side up, and opt for a long string to cover it.

Step 3. Use straight pins to secure the string and lay another one down, with its right side facing down. Align the edges of the two strings, but let the second one stretch out a bit. Sew the aligned edges.

Step 4. Press the string to set the seam allowance.

Step 5. Flip out the right side of the string. Press and turn over the block to trim excess fabric or thread.

Step 6. Join another string, but align its right edge with the first string's unsewn edge, and start sewing the ¼" seam allowance.

Step 7. Turn up the right side of the second string. Press and trim excess fabric and thread and continue to add other strings.

Step 8. Iron-press the string quilt.

Hand Quilting

Handcrafted quilts are gorgeous and unique, and you can create them without sewing machines. People often ask for these quilts because they appear tender, beautiful, and natural. To design these natural quilts, you only need a few simple guides. After we go through the process, you'll be fine to start making your own handcrafted quilts.

Required Materials

- A pair of scissors.

- An iron.

- "Between" needles (short needles with small eyes).

- Quilt frame or hoop.

- Cotton threads.

- Safety pins.

Instructions

Step 1. Arrange and Baste Your Quilt Sandwich—Press the top of your quilt to open and flatten the seams. Face down, spread the quilt on a clean surface and tape or pin its edges firmly to the surface.

Place the batting over the quilt, but make sure it's spread on the quilt evenly. Also, bumps and wrinkles on the batting must be eliminated. Lay the quilt face-up on the batting and press the quilt back to split the fabric into three layers.

Pin the three layers from the middle of the quilt downward. Be sure the quilt is smooth and free of wrinkles, and you may want to hold them with safety pins. Make sure the space between the two pins is less than four inches.

You can use large stitches to hold the layers, but the space between two stitch lines must not exceed four inches. Trim the batting and backing on the edge a bit to keep them under two inches.

Step 2. Place the Quilt in the Hoop or Frame—Quilt the middle section before you deal with the edges to align the layers. Gently pull the quilt to prevent overstretching the fabric. You might pull the fabric out of shape if you do not handle the quilt with care.

Step 3. Thread the Needle—Avoid tangled threads if you want to speed up the process. Instead, start with 18" thread. As soon as you thread your needle, tie a knot at the end of the thread and trim it. Stitch the batting and quilt top from the top downward, but don't go near the backing. Opt for any thread you want, but make sure the color of the thread matches your fabric.

Step 4. Begin Quilting—Make up-and-down stitching lines at even intervals on the fabric. Again, these lines should be straight and normal stitches. Per inch, feel free to make at least four stitches.

Stabilize the surface by placing one of your hands below the quilt sandwich while you are quilting. Carefully pull the needle through the quilt to avoid piercing your skin. Be mindful of the layout and make sure the stitches are smooth and neat.

Add more stitches to beautify the quilt, but make sure the stitches add value to the quilt.

Step 5. Add Final Touches—Take your time to examine the quilt to ensure that everything appears smooth and unique. Trim excess thread or fabric from the edges of the quilt before you join the binding.

Chapter Four:
Marking and Stencils

To Use a Stencil or Not?

You still need to remember the rule: practice and experiment. There are many quilters out there who make great free-motion quilts from patterns in their head. If you want to avoid the stencil and marker, then you need to work at committing the design into your head so thoroughly that you anticipate every move. With practice, this is possible. Besides, working with no markings will also reduce the beginner's pressure, thus helping remove jitters and avoid visible mistakes. There is something about following a line that makes some people's hands shake and vision a little blurry. If you can practice quilting without the lines, it would help reduce the pressure and allow your hand to follow your head.

Feel free to draw stencils on your projects but know that you don't need to follow the lines perfectly. Everything takes practice, and over time, you should be able to follow the lines seamlessly. After all, those lines marking the stencils are not permanent. Take control of your project and work at your pace, focusing on improving each time.

Use of Stencils

So, you have an idea of what patterns to quilt and are excited about starting? Well, before you even touch that quilt, consider drawing your masterpiece on a piece of paper to see what it would look like. However, if you are quite confident in your design, then you can draw it on the quilt itself. Whatever you choose, do not start stitching before you have drawn that design and loved the outcome.

One of the positives of using stencils is that you can use them even after basting the quilt. Sometimes, you may need to trace the chosen design onto the top of the quilt using a light box before basting. The choice of what to do lies in your hands. Remember that in free-motion quilting, you hold the control.

Your choice of a stencil can make your quilting work difficult. The best stencils for free-motion quilting are continuous lines. Occasionally, you could come across a stencil that calls for starting and stopping in different places. Although such a design is good for hand quilting, it may be challenging for machine quilting. By adding a curve or loop, it is still possible to create a continuous line, however, though it is easier to stitch without stopping and starting so often.

Marking

The market today offers many markers. You will need those marks to wash away and leave no trace of their existence on your quilt. Therefore, it is best to pick out your marker carefully. Although it may seem convenient to pick out anything that leaves a mark, you do not want to ruin your fabric or leave ugly marks.

Types of Markers

There are different types of markers that you can use to mark or transfer the design onto your quilt. These include:

1. **Chalk Pencil/Marker**—Also known as pen style chaco liner, though most people now refer to it as the chalk pen, marker, or pencil. Chalk remains a popular choice, and has been for a long time.

   You, however, need to be careful when using chalk; make sure to carry out a swatch test and don't press too hard into the fabric. You may have challenges washing the chalk off certain fabrics. Also, when using a chalk pen, it is best not to stack fabric together because the chalk may rub onto those other fabrics, causing smudges to appear on your carefully drawn lines. You need clear lines to ease your movement during quilting.

   You can opt for contrasting chalk pen colors to improve visibility.

2. **Quilt Pounce**—The quilt pounce is the "cool kid" of quilting markers. Here, you would use a pounce pad to transfer stencils onto the fabric. You run the pounce pad over the fabric to transfer it, much like the traditional ink and stamp. This saves you much time used in tracing patterns. The method is also simple and accurate.

3. **Water-Soluble Pencils**—As the name suggests, they dissolve in water. They are pretty stylish pencils that come in a wide selection of colors so you can choose what works well with your type of fabric.

   As a cautionary measure, it is important to test the marker over time, heat, and water to make sure you do not have a situation of resurrecting marked lines. On some occasions, marks may become visible after some time or with exposure to heat.

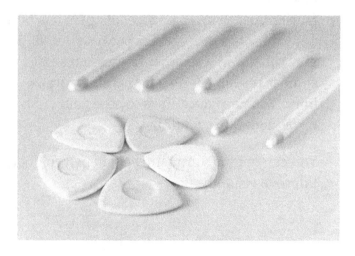

4. **Hera Marker**—Resembles a dull butter knife and is a favorite of many quilters. The Hera marker has a smooth finish and works by creating a crease in the quilt without snagging the fabric. There is no single mark left on the fabric, meaning that you need not worry about ruining it, or if it will wash off cleanly. The crease offers a subtle guideline for you to follow while quilting. If you want straight lines, you would simply pair it with a ruler and make the best straight lines without leaving marks on your beautiful fabric.

5. **Air and Water-Soluble Pens**—If you do not want to start washing off markings, then this is just what you need. The ink seems to disappear in thin air—literally. All you would do is mark, stitch, and the ink is gone! Although this option may be advantageous, it's likely not a good idea if you have small children who need your attention or are easily distracted. By the time you turn back on your quilt, the markings could all be gone, and you would have to start from scratch.

6. **Graphite Pencil**—You can use a normal graphite pencil to mark your work, but you would have to be careful of leftover marks. If you have a heavy hand, you may want to steer away from a graphite pencil. The best way to use it is to make light marks. Always do a test; there are many instances when the pencil won't

wash off, forcing you to invent a new pattern or make do with the ruined one.

7. **Frixion Erasable Pen**—Originally, this pen was not intended to be used by crafters or quilters, but as humans, we like to experiment. Since the ink "disappears," a few of us thought it would be a great tool for marking quilts. Despite the packaging calling it erasable, in reality, it is not erasable, but thermo-sensitive. The ink disappears when heated, and you should expect it to reappear when cooled. In terms of physics, matter doesn't exactly disappear; it merely changes form. This is the same concept.

   In some instances when used on a dark fabric, the lines may appear ghosted upon heat application. You need to be aware that Frixion pens contain permanent ink, so, although it may disappear, it will not wash out fully from your fabric.

   With the many available options, it is best to keep this pen away from your quilts.

8. **Masking tape:** Yes, even a masking tape can get the markings done. There are quilting masking tapes that you can use to mark your patterns. If you do not have a marking tool, you can simply borrow some children's masking tape and get marking. Of course, it will not be

pretty initially, but it will serve its purpose, all with no marks on your fabric.

The added advantage is that you do not need an entire roll—you can use the same piece multiple times because it doesn't have to be super sticky; it just has to hold on to the fabric. Additionally, tape is thick enough to see, so you will not struggle with trying to guess on faint lines.

However, as expected, it is difficult to do any other lines aside from straight ones. You will also have to discard a wad of tape by the end, even after re-using the pieces. In this sense, it is not an eco-friendly option.

What to Remember When Using Marking Tools

a. **Read and Follow the Manufacturer's Guidelines on Use**—Most times, we assume that we know how to do things. Who wouldn't know how to use a pen to trace out some stencils? Or with a ruler to draw a straight line? It sounds easy, but it is necessary to read the user instructions.

Have you ever struggled to open food packaging, only for it to fly all over, with the packaging clearly saying where to cut? Some marking tools may need to be used in certain conditions, like temperature and in the absence of moisture. You could easily ruin your fabric and pour your work down the drain by not following the instructions labeled on the marking pen.

b. **Run a test**—You must do a test on every fabric you intend to use before the actual markings. If it says to wash, wash and see if the markings remain. That one minute of testing can save you from ruining an entire project, considering your investment in it. Delay your urge to get right into it and do a test. The point is to test first on a small piece.

c. **Press Lightly and Not Too Hard**—You can definitely press too hard on the fabric. The simple difference between pressing and applying too much pressure could result in damage. When using pencils or pens with fine tips, pressing too hard could cause holes in the fabric. If using markers, pressing too much could lead to bloating or lines so thick that you can stitch in a straight line. If your markers are dry, replace them; don't test your strength on the quilt.

Instead of marking the designs directly onto the fabric, you could use quilting paper to prevent exposing your quilt to chemicals from the markers.

Chapter Summary

In this chapter, we have looked at the use of stencils and markers and learned that:

- There are different markers available for use on the market, including water-soluble pens, chalks, graphite pencils, quilt pounce, and hera markers, among others

- Choose your marker according to your fabric.

- Always remember to test your marker to ensure it washes off.

- Opt for stencils with continuous lines for ease of free-motion quilting.

In the next chapter, you will learn how to prepare your machine for free-motion quilting.

Chapter Five:
Preparation of Quilting Machine

Congratulations on getting here! You have all the basics at hand and have done shopping for your quilting material. If you have a new machine, now is the time to get rid of all those coverings and get her to work. If you pulled out your mother's grandmother's machine, dust it off and let us have fun quilting.

Having a machine is one thing and setting it up is another. Although you can get your quilting machine ready in a matter of a few minutes, it is important to ensure that you do it properly; otherwise, you subject yourself to frustration. For a beginner, the task may seem daunting, and you will probably be worried about getting things wrong. Relax—quilting is an activity that you should enjoy, so let us set up in simple steps.

How to Get Your Machine Ready

a. **Clean and Oil**—For new machines, this may not be necessary, but if the machine had been used before, you should clean and oil it. The stitch rate for quilting is quite high—about 1000 stitches per minute—often resulting in lint building up in the bobbin case. Frequent cleaning is necessary to keep your bobbin case free from loose thread and lint. You should also oil the hook to keep it in good working condition and make stitching easier.

Your machine comes with a brush for the cleaning task. Alternatively, you can use a toothbrush or stiff paint brush. Remove the bobbin case and brush it off on the inside, making sure to brush every inch, including the tension spring and ring. While you are at it, it is also a good time to inspect for burrs and sweep out the feed dog. Once clean, you can put one drop of clear quilting machine oil on the race. Remember to sew first on a waste piece of the cloth to absorb any excess oil before beginning a new project.

b. **Thread the Bobbin/Spool**—They say failing to plan is planning to fail. The case here could be true; you need to prepare adequately for free-motion quilting. Besides, once you get the hang of it, you will not want to stop. Thread your bobbins and prepare your spools. The key is to ensure that you have a considerable amount of thread to get you started. About three full bobbins are ideal for getting the project off the ground.

c. **Fasten a Straight-Stitch Plate**—Unlike the standard stitch plate, the straight stitch plate comes with a smaller opening that offers more support to the quilt and prevents it from getting pushed into the opening of the needle. It also creates beautiful quilting stitches.

d. **Put in a New Needle**—With your newly acquired knowledge on needles, choose whichever one matches your project. You can change the needle whenever you need to.

e. **The Quilting Foot**—If you opted to have a quilting foot, ensure that it is attached and ready for use. You will want to move your fabric freely and enjoy great visibility.

f. **Lower the Feed Dogs**—Since you are now in control of every stitch, its direction, and its speed, the feed dogs can take a well-deserved break. Depending on your machine's type, there are various mechanisms of lowering them. Follow your manual's instructions to lower the feed dogs, which will sometimes be as simple as pressing a button. Alternatively, you can set the stitch length to zero, which should keep the feed dogs in their original position so you can take charge.

g. **Needle Down**—When you set the needle down feature, you ensure that every time the machine stops, the needle is down into the fabric. This helps you manage the fabric easily by keeping an uninterrupted line of stitching when adjusting quilt position.

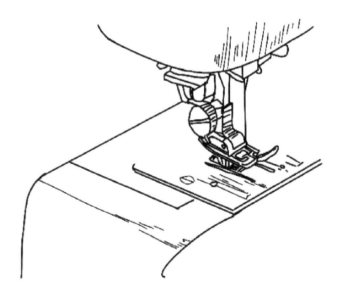

h. **Thread Your Machine**—Depending on your machine, the threading process may vary, but the basics will be similar. Refer to your machine's user manual. Here, we will look at the basics, and in case your machine needs more, you can always refer to the instructions that come with it or look online.

- Take the thread, and at the top of your machine, you will find a spool pin; that is where you will put your thread. Once you have put it in, the thread should be able roll and unfold easily when you pill it anticlockwise.

- Put the thread through the top loop and pull it down gently toward the tension loop.

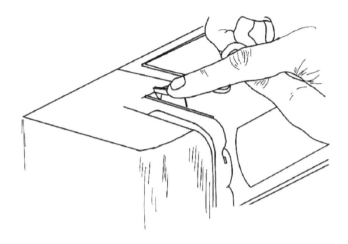

- You don't want the thread unfolding; use one hand to hold the spool in place as you pull it down. You can now press the thread down and through the cut-out to fit snugly into the tension discs.

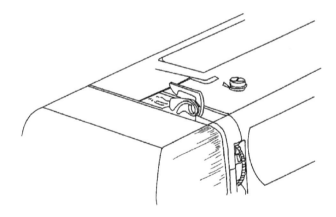

- Once secured, take it around the bottom of the next loop and pull it back up.

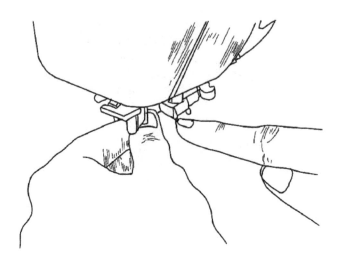

- Pass it through the notch hole, whose work is to pull the thread up and down. If you cannot find it, use your hand wheel by turning it toward you or your foot pedal to reveal it.

- Pill the thread through the cut-out again.

- Pass it through the hook situated above your needle.

- Insert the thread though the needle eye.

i. **Stitch a Sample**—Now is the time to test your machine to ensure everything is working together. Stitch a sample to test the thread tension, needle feel, and general workings of the machine. If there are any issues, go through the process again and adjust any step that you may have missed. That is why you have this guide; you can always come refer to it again.

j. **Adjust the Tension**—If the tension feels off, your machine has settings for adjusting that. You can increase or lower depending on the thread, patterns, and humidity. Free-motion quilting involves a little more pulling and tagging, uses different threads, and is generally more free. You may not want so much tension; play around with different tension settings to find the right one.

k. **All Set!**—The quilt is an empty canvas, and you an enthusiastic quilter. The time is now. Beginner jitters exist, but always remember that even the greatest quilters started somewhere and on a day like today. Embrace the "free" in free-motion quilting, make your patterns and mistakes, and enjoy the process.

Placing Your Machine Right

You want maximum comfort when quilting. There is a high possibility that you will spend many hours on the activity because, once you get the hang of it, you may not want to stop. Therefore, you will need your machine positioned comfortably and in a way that prevents aches and minimizes mistakes. Here are some tips you should consider:

a. Place your machine on a large, flat table with a cut-out place to secure it. Ensure your machine is safe, secure, and not moving around, so you can quilt without any worries of the machine slipping, moving, or falling off. You also want the feeling of being grounded and in control.

b. Give your quilting table a back support, preferably from a wall. It is important to keep it in place and prevent your quilt from falling from the other side.

c. Place your workstation in a well-lit environment. Remember that you want those patterns coming out beautifully; visibility is crucial. Besides, working in a poorly lit environment will put a strain on your eyes.

d. Working in a clean environment will enable you to focus on the task without interruptions. Clean your working and extension tables well to remove smudge marks and any other dirt that may be there. Your quilt will slide smoothly on a clean surface and make your quilting more efficient.

e. Have a large working space and extend your working table, if needed. You will want a surface that fits the whole quilt without some of it hanging off the side. Even a small corner of the quilt hanging over the edge could mean an unnecessary pull and potentially bend the needle, making it thump into the throat plate and break. You can prevent such accidents by extending your work surface. You can put a table, bookcase, or any other surface that is of similar height adjacent to your machine to extend your working area.

Chapter Summary

Preparing your machine for quilting is a prerequisite condition for efficient and fun quilting. You need to ensure that:

- You clean and oil your machine, thread your bobbin, attach a stitch-plate, attach a quilting foot, put in a new needle, lower the feed dog, and thread the machine. Once ready, you need to adjust the tension and stitch a sample to make sure everything is working well.

- Place your machine in an environment that is conducive for quilting. Your machine should have the necessary support, and the environment should be well-lit and clean.

- Quilting is a relaxing and enjoyable activity, so create the right mood for it.

In the next chapter, you will learn how to make your quilt sandwich easily, including tips to help with your basting experience.

Chapter Six:
Baste Your Quilt

Quilting involves layering fabrics. Usually, there are mainly three layers: a woven top cloth, a layer of wadding or batting, and woven cloth at the back. The three layers would be sewn together through quilting. How you set up these layers is of utmost importance and determines how the final product will look .

Before you begin quilting, you have to place the layers correctly together and hold them together temporarily. The process is referred to as basting, and it is crucial in determining your outcome. Remember that all the layers have to be smooth and wrinkle-free. You have to make sure there are no puckers, since they restrict the flow of your quilt under the presser foot.

You need to ensure that you choose the right batting for your quilt because such also determines the general outlook and type of finishing. Let us choose our batting, and then we can baste.

Choosing the Batting

Have you seen all quilt waddings available on the market? It can be overwhelming. However, variety is the spice of life, and we should appreciate that we have the ability to choose. There are two main factors to consider when choosing a wadding: loft and fiber.

Loft—This simply implies the thickness or thinness of your batting. A low loft is thin, whereas a high loft would be thick. In other words, a low loft wadding would make a thinner quilt, whereas a high loft batting will give you a thicker comforter.

Fiber—Refers to the material that makes the quilt. In most cases, the batting is made of cotton, polyester, or a blend of cotton and polyester. Each of these materials has its advantages. For instance, polyester is lightweight, less expensive, and durable; however, it tends to shift if not quilted densely. Cotton, on the other hand, is light and breathable, offers the heaviest weight for batting, and is best for machine quilting. Your cotton batting will also wash well without pilling and shrink slightly. The cotton blend is usually made up of 80% cotton and 20% polyester. As it is not pure cotton, it is less-expensive and will not shrink as much.

The batting—mainly cotton and cotton blend—may come with scrim, which is a thin sheet of stabilizer on one or either side of the wadding that prevents separation or stretching of the fibers. Scrim makes the batting strong and stable, thus making your basting process easier.

Researching your batting is quite important. Manufacturers, in most cases, give guidelines on how far apart the stitches should be for each batting. Having this information is important to ensure that you make a quality quilt. You should always strive to adhere to the manufacturer's recommendations.

The Basting Process

Preparation is crucial. You can make your work easier by having all the items you need at hand. It will also save you time, since you won't be running around looking for items.

What to have at hand:

1. Top cover.

2. Bottom cover.

3. Batting.

4. Iron box.

5. General purpose masking tape.

6. Lint roller.

7. Dog pins.

8. Quick clip tool.

9. Safety Pins/spray baste.

Process of Basting

Step 1. Smoothen the Back Cover—Start by ironing the backing fabric. You want it to be smooth and without any wrinkles. Now that your quilt is ready for use, place it on a flat surface, face down. You can use your floor, an area with cleared out space, or even a large working table. Ensure there is enough room, so it is all spread out and taut *without* stretching.

Step 2. Hold it in Place—Using the masking tape, hold the back fabric in place by taping it on the surface. The surface has to be hard and flat to prevent it from moving or wrinkling. If you are using a smaller surface than you quilt, and it ends up hanging off the sides, you can use your dog pins to hold them in place. If possible, avoid a situation where your quilt has to fold.

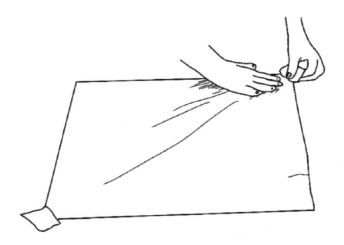

Step 3. Place Your Batting—Once your back quilt is well-placed, you can then place your batting. Lay down the batting carefully on top of the bottom cover and smoothen it. You can use a lint roller to remove any lint or threads that may be there. The surface should be clean. You can then use your hands to smoothen the surface and get rid of any puckers.

Step 4. Clip Them—You do not have to clip them together, but it helps to solemnize their union. You can use a dog clip to hold them together.

Step 5. Place the Top—Add the top quilt and smoothen it out so it fits well on the batting. Ensure that there are no wrinkles. You can add as many layers as you please, but remember that the more you add, the more difficult it becomes to hold them together. You should see batting material.

Step 6. Baste—The time is now to join the layers together. You can use a basting spray, which is available in stores. You must, however, ensure that what you get easily washes out. The use of basting spray calls for a well-ventilated room because it is harmful to breathe in. Unfortunately, it can also leave deposits on the floor that are hard to remove.

Alternatively, you can use basting pins. They are slightly curved, unlike regular safety pins, making it easy to pin through the three layers. Using the quick clip tool, insert safety pins to hold the layers together. The best way to do this is to start at the center and place pins every few inches as you move toward the edge. As you place the pins, you must be careful that you do not leave any pucker; you want a smooth finish, ready for quilting. Ensure that the edges also have pins in place.

If you don't like either the spray or the pins, you can use thread basting, which involves making large stitches by hand. Plastic tags can replace basting pins and are usually pushed through the layers using a gun-like tool.

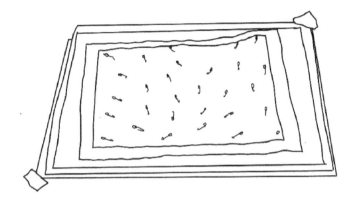

Step 7. Remove the Tape—When the pins are in place, remove the tape and check that everything is flat and tight. If you find puckers, excess fabric, or looseness, now is the time to fix it. You certainly will not like adjusting puckers after you start stitching. You can use a fabric with a busy pattern to help hide your beginner mistakes.

Basting Tips

Store Your Pins Open—We tend to close our pins instinctively, even safety pins. Resist the temptation to close all those pins and instead, store them in a box while open. Think about it—when you need to use the pins, you will have to open them, and when you remove them, they will be open. Isn't it better to leave them open? For safety's sake, you will need to keep the box closed and in a safe place;

otherwise, leave the pins open. It will save you basting time during your next project.

Embrace the Kwik Klip—This simple wooden tool will save your hands much wear and tear when closing all those pins.

Use the Tiles—If you have a tiled floor, you can use the lines to keep your quilt centered and layers straight.

Don't Stretch the Fabric—The fabric needs to be taut but not stretched. If you stretch it, it will likely lose its shape, which is not what you want.

Cover Your Work Area—If you are using a basting spray, you need to cover the surface you are working on prior to application. The spray can get messy and leave residue. Besides, covering the surface will mean no need to clean up afterwards.

Iron the Fabric—Ironing the fabric will leave you with a smooth and wrinkle-free starting point that will make your basting work easier.

Chapter Summary

Basting is an important part of the quilting process, and although challenging for some, it gets better with practice. What you need to remember is:

- Your choice of batting is important; choose one that fits your purpose.

- Ensure that the fabric is taut without being stretched.

- Iron the fabric to prevent wrinkles.

- Smoothen as you baste to avoid puckering.

In the next chapter, you will start on your first stitches.

Chapter Seven:
The First Stitches

As you switch on your machine, and take a seat with your basted quilt, you can be certain that from the first stitch, you cannot expect perfection, but you will at least continue to improve. Do not feel alone, overwhelmed, or intensely nervous—you are in safe hands. In this guide, we will walk through the first stitches to ensure that you do not go through unnecessary trial and error.

Choose your needle carefully and thread depending on your fabric. If you are a bit uncertain on how to do so, you can revisit chapter two of this guide. Remember that your choice of needle and thread is crucial in making your stitching easy and efficient. Before then, let us prepare adequately.

What to Keep in Mind

Large Working Area—If your project is big, then you will need a large working surface on your machine's rear and left sides to support the quilt's weight adequately. Failure to do so can result in your machine being pulled off by the weight of the quilt.

Roll Your Basted Quilt—Rolling your quilt will help make your work easier. After basting, spread your sandwich on the floor and roll from either side toward the center. You can secure the sides with bicycle clips or safety pins.

Start from the Center—When quilting, it is best to start stitching from the center and move toward the edges. This will help keep your sandwich intact and prevent puckers. Additionally, it is easier to balance the weight of the quilt this way.

Remove the Pins—If you basted using pins, remove them as you approach. Do not stitch over the pins, as it becomes harder to remove them and can interfere with your stitches. They can also result in accidents. The pins can cause your needle to break, and those fragments could end up in your eyes. Quilting is a fun activity, so don't turn it into a risky affair.

Use Rubber Finger Tips—If you have trouble moving the quilt around or have dry fingers, you can cover them with rubber finger tips, which are available in most stores that stock office supplies.

Rubber finger tips will give you a better grip of the quilt, enabling you to move it easily.

Remember that your sewing speed combined with how fast you move the quilt will determine the length of your stitches.

Start Slow and Steady—The key to beautiful quilting is maintaining a steady machine speed and pairing that with smooth fabric movement.

What You Need

- 2 threads (1 for needle, 1 for bobbin).

- Needle, according to thread.

Steps

1. Check for disengaged feed dogs and an inserted darning foot. Your machine is ready for use, but a minute or two of checking through it can save you much frustration and many mistakes. You have to make sure you disengage the feed dogs to gain control of the process. Also, make sure the darning foot is inserted and ready.

2. Once you are certain that everything else is on point, including having adequate thread, you are then ready to stitch.

3. Position your sandwich on top of the feed dogs, placing it in a way that the center of the quilt or spot you wish to stitch first lies directly under

the needle. Ideally, you should ensure the quilt has a good balance and is well-supported as you begin. Place your hands on either side of the quilt—about two inches from the presser foot—and you can then use them to guide the quilt as you wish.

4. Adjust the tension by pulling the bobbin thread. You need the right tension from the start and may need to place the presser either up or down, depending on the level of tension you need.

5. Do a half stitch to pop the bobbin thread out.

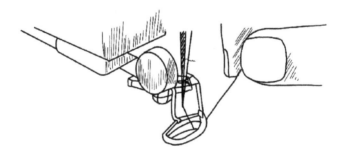

1. Hold both the bobbin thread and needle thread and pull them to maintain the tension. You want to ensure that you do not lose the tension you have already adjusted, and that you are all set to allow the needle and thread to meet the fabric.

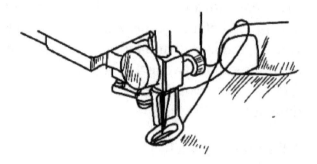

2. As you begin to stitch, remember that the first two stitches are very important. You have to secure them to prevent the subsequent work from coming off. To secure them, sew two stitches forward, then two stitches back. The front and back stitching ensures that your stitches remain secured. You can then continue with your free-motion quilting.

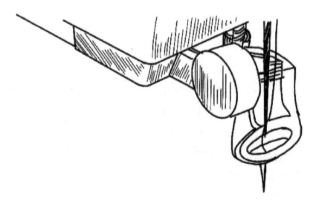

3. Make sure you don't stitch the same spot more than once. Doing so will create a knot at that particular spot and could possibly damage your

fabric. On occasion though, you can stitch more than once.

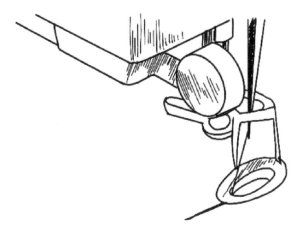

4. As you stitch, guide the fabric with both hands and move it so the needle traces the marked designs or lines. You will most likely not achieve perfection today, but keep up the right attitude and practice, and you will be proficient in no time.

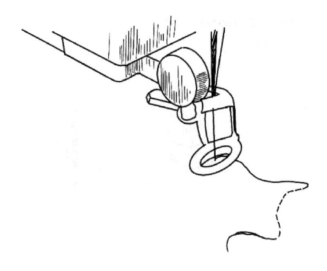

5. The secret to great free-motion quilting is moving your fabric slowly but smoothly while keeping the machine's speed steady. Moving too fast or slow could result in gaps and a mix of overly long or short stitches. Keep it slow and steady.

6. Quilting can take a toll on anyone, particularly beginners who may not be happy with the results. Be kind to yourself. These are your first stitches—much like a baby's first steps, you need to celebrate them, despite being a few and most likely not of high quality. Enjoy the lack of rules that come with free-motion quilting. You do not even need to follow any pattern; just let your imagination work for you and keep practicing.

7. Choose a small project to start with, like a pillowcase or table cloth. Everyone likes to finish a project, whether big or small. Seeing a completed project, no matter how small, will serve as encouragement to continue quilting.

Five Items to Have Handy

Before starting any quilting project, you will want to be adequately prepared. You certainly do not want to begin the quilting process and have to stop in the middle because you cannot cut your fabric into the desired size. To ensure the quilting experience is smooth and enjoyable, here are some items that you will need to have at hand.

1. Scissors

There are tons of different types of scissors available on the market. However, your key focus when looking for a pair of scissors for your quilting is on the sharpness of the blade and hand comfort. You need scissors that you can use without developing sore hands and ones that fit your hand well. While looking at the blade sharpness, you also have to keep in mind your environment. Blades made of stainless steel will not maintain a sharp edge for a long time but will resist rusting. On the other hand, high-carbon steel blades, although they do not offer good rust resistance, will keep a sharp edge.

If you do not buy any other scissors, you will definitely have to get some professional fabric scissors. Using all-purpose scissors could leave you with frayed edges or jagged cuts and very tired hands. The task can become a nightmare when you need to cut curves.

Ideally, you should have at least a high-quality pair of shears to use with long cuts; for the small cuts, you will want a good pair of scissors. With the two, you can focus on the creative process instead of the frustration. For ease of identification, scissors are short in size, usually with a total length of no more than ten inches. Shears are longer with a length of over ten inches. Most quilters opt for 12-inch shears, which are ideal for cutting long lengths of material and offer long, straight cuts.

A fabric scissors helps to easily snip the fabric. They mostly come with a curve handle, which improves the accuracy when cutting on flat surfaces. The pointed tips help with precision. A key tip to maintaining the sharpness of the blade is to avoid using the scissors on anything else other than your fabric.

2. Needles

You definitely know that you need a needle, and you have to choose one carefully according to the thread you are using and fabric you intend to stitch. However, what you may not know is that you need to have more needles available and not at the store, but within reach. Accidents happen, needles break, some become blunt faster than you expected, and others deliver below your expectations. You certainly do not want to stop your project to go to the store for a needle.

A crafts store will yield various types of needles. When possible, get a good number of assorted needles to allow a variety to test on, and choose whenever you need one. A general recommendation is to start your quilting with a fresh needle each time, but many quilters use theirs until it is blunt or broken. Whichever kind of a quilter you are, you will still need a fresh needle at some point, so having some at hand will be important.

3. Thread

There is no stitching without thread, and most projects do take up a lot of thread; you will need to be prepared. You may need a particular thread for each project, but cotton tends to be all-purpose. You can opt to stock up on a variety, depending on the kind of quilts you intend to make, or buy for each project. Thread also tends to run out very fast during stitching. You can also get assorted threads to keep at hand. Whatever you do, ensure that your choice of thread is high-quality; you do not want it to break easily. Besides, thread is what gives quilting its beauty, so do not allow your efforts to be lost because of the thread.

4. Pins

Quilting involves joining three or more layers together, and for that, you need pins to hold the fort before you can do the actual stitching. You can use any kind of pins, but those with a large head will be ideal for ease of removal. For the basting process, it is best to use safety pins to avoid pricking when handling the sandwich. Get a good number of pins that allows you to baste more than one sandwich at a time. Do not forget to get a storage container to store them safely and avoid losing them.

5. Iron

When basting, it is best to iron your fabric before spreading it on the surface. An iron board is an essential item for any quilter. Ironing your fabric ensures you don't have wrinkles, which can ruin your quilt. Ironed fabric tends to come together easily and firmly, eliminating much shifting and easing the basting and stitching processes. With the iron, it is best to also get an ironing board or suitable ironing surface to do the job. You don't need anything fancy; your regular home iron and ironing board can do the job effectively.

Above are some of the most important items you need, other than the machine and fabric. Another item you should consider is a seam ripper because, although everyone makes mistakes and undoing seams is part of quilting, as a beginner, you will make *many* mistakes. Having a seam ripper at hand will quicken the process of undoing any poorly done seams, so you can get back to stitching. Other items include a tape measure to ensure your measurements are correct and a marking tool to help mark the designs.

Quilting Tips

Quilting is a learning process that calls for commitment. As a beginner, it can be easy to feel overwhelmed by what you don't know and the high expectations. Here are a few pointers to always keep in mind before starting any project.

1. Clean Your Machine

Your machine is your main tool in free-motion quilting, and you need to take care of it. One way of doing so is to clean it by de-fluffing the bobbin case and removing the throat plate. Ensure it is clean, then oil it. Ideally, you should clean and de-lint the machine after every project or every eight to ten hours of quilting. The machine will thank you by running well, and your stitches will look good without much trouble. Of course, it is necessary to get a good quality machine from a brand that lasts.

2. Threading

First of all, you should always use quality thread; it will not break easily, nor will it leave much lint on your machine. That said, many quilters struggle with threading. An easy way to thread is to use a small amount of hair spray on the thread before rolling it between your fingers and allowing it to dry for a few seconds. The hairspray will stiffen the thread, and with a snip of the edge, you can easily poke it through the machine and needle. Alternatively, you can put a white piece of paper behind the needle to improve the visibility of its eye. If that does not appeal to you, cut your thread at a 45-degree angle to make it easy to thread.

You should ensure your spool holder is oriented correctly, so the thread can run smoothly. In most cases, the machine will come with two spool holders—a vertical and a horizontal one. The easiest way to know is by checking how the thread is wound up. Threads that are straight should go on the vertical spool holder, whereas those that form an X are best placed on the horizontal one.

3. Needle

Always use the appropriate needle, as per your project and thread. Using the wrong needle can result in breakage or frustration from inefficient quilting. Sometimes, you may need to change your needle. In that case, it is best to place it back in the container but place it the opposite way from the new needles. You can place it with the point upwards, indicating to you which one is the used needle. Also, if your machine starts to skip stitches, it is time to change your needle and clean up the bobbin case.

4. Fabric Cutting

Invest in a good, solid pair of scissors, and don't lose it—it will be one of your most important assets. Keep it for its chosen purpose and do not yield to the temptation to snip on a piece of paper with them. If you can, get a different pair of scissors for silk.

You should always measure twice to be certain. Remember that cutting cannot be undone. Also, ensure that you add an extra inch to the edge of the quilt; that way, you can easily stitch close to where the binding will be done.

If you are struggling with making your fabric taut but not stretch and achieving a wrinkle-free finish, try spray basting. For the smoothness in the curves, a key tip is to use many pins, each taking only a small bite of the fabric.

5. Stitching

Remember that in free-motion stitching, you are the one in control. Find a good room to quilt in with adequate lighting and make it your happy place.

You may struggle to quilt lines with a good level of accuracy. When possible, I hold my ruler with both hands for added stability. I can easily go around a curve while holding the ruler in both hands. I like to have some of my fingers on the ruler and some on the fabric, since it helps give me a sense of grounding. However, there is still a high chance that the stitches will be uneven. Aim for consistency, and you will see tangible results.

No matter how bad you think the quilt is, finish it. There is a sense of satisfaction in finishing a project, even if it looks imperfect. Embrace those ugly stitches—they are how you work to get more even and beautiful stitches.

Chapter Summary

Your first stitches will always remain some of the most memorable ones, mostly because they are also likely to be some of the most ugly ones. Remember that:

- Whatever you do, make sure you quilt; you can only get better.

- Always take on small projects first and finish them.

- Quilting is an experience; learn through the stitches.

- Always secure your first stitches by double stitching them so they do not run.

- Be kind to yourself and enjoy the process.

In the next chapter, you will learn about tension, which is one of the most important things that affect the quilting journey. Tension can make or break your thread, so you will need to know when and how to adjust it.

Chapter Eight:
Tension

Finding the right tension is crucial for creating beautiful stitches during free-motion quilting. On the flip side, get it wrong, and you end up with ugly stitches and loops. Your confidence level when it comes to tension may be low, but this is free-motion quilting. Here, anything is possible. Besides, you have this guide to help you through the process.

Needle-Thread Tension

Let us address the top tension first. If you remember, during threading, we talked about putting your thread through discs and ensuring it is secured properly. Top tension refers to the tension that emanates from the discs found at the front of your machine, which in turn affects the needle thread. In an ideal tension situation, there is a neutral tug of war between the top and bottom stitch, with the twist of the thread falling in the middle of the batting.

Tension Troubleshooting Tips

As with anything else, preparation is key. You do not want to spend hours adjusting tension without success simply because you and your machine are not ready. Hence, it is important to ensure that you:

- Have a needle that is oriented correctly to your machine; a fresh one would be ideal.

- Check that there is no lint in your machine. Lint could contribute to tension issues.

- Do not forget the presser foot. You will need to raise it when adjusting tension, but lower it when it is time to sew.

- Coordinate the needle size correctly to the thread size. For example, you can pair a thread of 40 weight with a needle of size 90/14.

- Use good quality thread; check for age and quality.

- Check the way the thread winds onto the bobbin. If it is wound in a crisscross, you may need to lift it off the spool and string through the machine.

- Thread your bobbin correctly; that is, evenly and with good pressure.

Adjusting Tension

To adjust tension, you need to raise the presser foot, and on a digital machine, select either a higher or lower number, depending on whether you want it tight or loose. If you are using an analog machine and lack the option to select numbers, all you have to do is turn the knob to either tighten or loosen it. You would then lower the presser foot, stitch, and check to see if everything is working as it should. Always remember that a high number means a higher tension, whereas a smaller number means reduced tension. When adjusting the tension, it is best to reduce or increase by half a number and test it out until it is right. Here is a more elaborate method of adjusting tension.

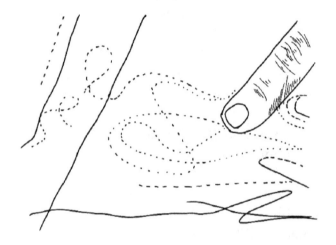

Thread Needle Thread (TNT) Method

Thread

Completely re-thread your machine from the spool. You can refer to your machine's manual for specifics on threading or online if you don't have the manual. You should make sure your threading is done as recommended by the manufacturer to avoid any errors. Once done, do a few stitches and check for the quality. If not, move to the needle.

An important point to note is that you cannot have proper tension without threading your machine correctly. The tension discs, thread guides, tension regulator, and bobbin-case spring all work together to ensure simultaneous flow of tread from the bobbin and the needle, allowing for the production of a symmetrical stitch.

To avoid any further tension issues due to the thread spool, you can use a thread stand. It will keep the tension even by creating a constant tension on the thread spool.

Needle

Now it's time to change the needle. Earlier, we discussed how to choose the appropriate needle. Choose one and replace what was already there. A top stitch needle is a good option, but ensure that the needle size matches the thread size.

Tension

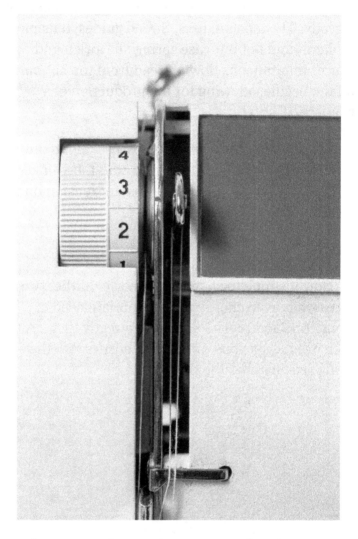

Always start by turning your machine's tension controls to zero and practice with a similar sandwich to the actual project to see if the tension is alright. Have the darning foot on and stitch for about half a minute and check if it works fine. If it is not, increase the tension and try again until you get the desired results.

When adjusting the tension, it is best to deal with one variable at a time; that way you can predict the outcome and move to the next variable. Let's look at some common problems that call for adjusting the tension.

Common Problems Associated with Tension

1. Top Eyelashes

Eyelashes refer to extreme looping. If you have eyelashes at the top, it means that the top thread is pulling more to its side than the bottom one, and the tension is too tight. You can then adjust your tension to a lower number by selecting one on a digital machine or simply adjusting your machine knob to the left if you are using the analog version. You should pay extra attention to your stitches' center of swirls, which is where eyelashes are likely to hide.

2. Back Eyelashes

Having eyelashes on the back of the quilt is quite common. Chances are high that you will, at one point or another, end up with them. The inability to see at the back as you quilt is a major contributing factor. Quilters usually realize that the back has eyelashes *way* after doing a considerable amount of work. Sometimes, it is only as you take a well-deserved break and admire your work that you start to notice. If you end up with eyelashes on the back, it simply means that the tension at the top is too loose.

The solution is to tighten or increase your top tension by putting your machine on a higher number or adjusting your knob correctly if using an analog machine.

3. Floaters

Sometimes, the stitches can opt to float away. Instead of creating an eyelash, the thread may appear to be "floating" on the quilt's back, though you can, in some instances, feel some bumps, despite the top thread barely showing. You can eliminate such a problem by increasing the top tension to ensure nice stitches both at the back and on top of the quilt.

4. Broken Thread

Broken thread is also a common occurrence, even more than having eyelashes on top of the quilt. In most cases, it is as a result of the top tension being too tight, and a quick adjustment should resolve it. However, if that does not sort out the issue, look at other factors like the presence of a burr on your needle plate or foot and checking that the presser foot is not too high.

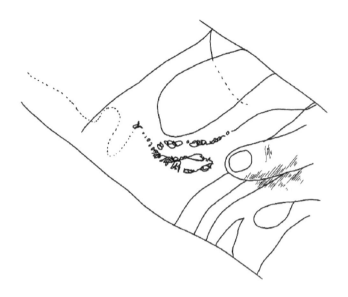

Having your tension too loose or too tight can make the rest of your work quite time-consuming. Although you may adjust your tension, the eyelashes and floaters are still on the quilt and call for unpicking. It is annoying and frustrating, but that is the only way to correct the stitches. To avoid such a situation, it is best to always check your tension.

When to Do the Tension Check

- **Before Any New Project**—After setting up your machine, adjust the tension and quilt a few stitches to make sure the tension is right.

- **Whenever You Go Back to Quilting**—If you leave your project lying around for some time—and it happens often—especially with all other responsibilities waiting, remember to check the tension.

- At the Start of a Thread Color, Bobbin, or Inserting a New Needle—Always ensure the new thread and needle are well-adjusted.

You may think that checking the tension will take much time and reduce your quilting time. Well, it will take a few moments and save you hours and frustration of unpicking down the road. Besides, the aim of quilting is to create a beautiful masterpiece, and tension plays a major role in that.

During tension testing, it is best to stitch some zigzags and loops because tension issues mainly show up at points and curves.

If you cannot clear your tension problems and can still see those little dots forming on either side of the quilt, still don't let that stop you from quilting. You can still use a camouflage quilt back, as there are occasionally problems that cannot be solved.

Chapter Summary

Getting the tension right is an important part of free-motion quilting.

- Remember to check for the correct tension before starting a stitch.

- Use the Thread-Needle-Tension method to get it just right.

- The thread and needle influence tension, but so do other factors, including the environment.

- You can start from zero tension and keep adjusting until you get the right stitches.

In the next chapter, you will actually get started. We will look at doodling and getting your project off the ground.

Chapter Nine:
Getting Started

Free-motion quilters have a saying that, "What is the top always stays at the top." In essence, this means that you do not need to do much flipping fabrics or twisting and turning. You only need to move your fabric as a whole in your direction of choice.

Let's look at how to free-motion quilt in a few steps.

Free-Motion Quilting Made Easy

1. **Prepare a Fabric Sandwich for Practice**—Since you have a good understanding of how to baste, you may enjoy the practice by making another sandwich— which could be relatively smaller—for you to test on. You have to test everything before actually quilting, lest it cost you hours and frustrate you.

   The practice sandwich should ideally be made from the same fabric as your project. It's not a waste of any new fabric; it is so that you can get the same feel and results as the main project.

   For example, if your project is made of cotton, and your practice sandwich is made of silk, the suitable thread and needle will differ. What will work on the sandwich may be horrendous on the actual project. To avoid that, make two sets of sandwiches using the same materials, one for the project and the other for the practice sandwich.

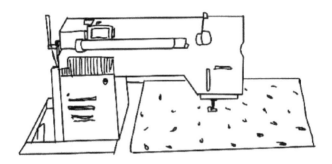

2. **Start Doodling**—Although you can find many patterns online, it is best to doodle yourself as you see fit. Like free-motion quilting, doodling does not come with a book of rules. You can move your quilt in any direction, which helps you set your wand. You can either let go and doodle freehand or make a particular pattern.

You can opt to start doodling from a piece of paper to gain confidence before shifting that to your practice sandwich. Some quilters develop a habit of doodling in a book during their free time to perfect their hand and come up with interesting patterns.

3. **Start with Doodling a Cursive L**—One of the simplest letters of the alphabet to write is L. Make fun of it by turning it into an entire pattern. There are many interesting ways to write the letter L, and your imagination is your only limit. Did you know you can even draw a bird out of a simple L? Everything is possible with doodling. You can also do the cursive C, which will prepare you for feather designs. Other letters of the alphabet can become some of the best patterns. Get your pen or pencil out and start doodling.

For free-motion quilting, it is best to use continuous lines. Draw without putting the pencil down; that way, you will also be able to quilt continuously without having to stop.

4. **Repeat**—Once you have made something that you like—an L, or any other pattern that you are satisfied with—repeat it until you can replicate the same pattern. You see why you need a paper? The goal is to have the pattern embedded in your brain. Most times, after a while, the brain may play tricks and tell you that you got it, only to begin making mistakes. Keep going for a long time to ensure that you *really* got it. Then, you can begin working on your practice sandwich.

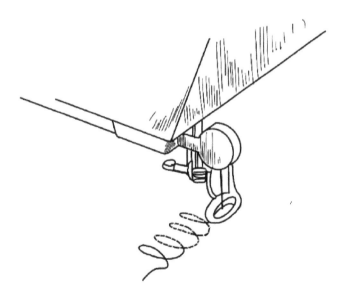

5. **Maintain a Certain Speed**—Once you have your doodle well-settled in a good space in your brain, it is time for speed. You want to

maintain a particular speed to keep your stitches even when quilting. Practice makes perfect. Keep practicing, but with a focus on doodling at a certain speed for each doodle.

6. **Match Your Movement Speed to Your Machine Speed**—How fast you move your fabric also depends on the speed of your machine. You need to strike a balance between the two; otherwise, moving one faster than the other can result in eyelashes and ugly looping. Remember that pushing hard on the machine will increase the speed considerably. Also, do not hurry over the top when doing sharp or curved designs, as it can result in a longer stitch length that could ruin your pattern. Keep playing with it, pushing on the foot pedal and moving your hands. The goal is not to do it too fast; this is not a race. What you are aiming for is consistency.

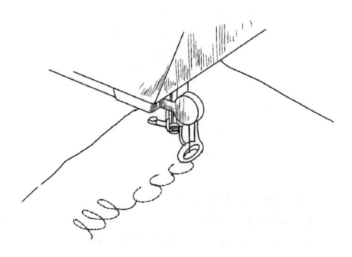

7. **Experiment with Threads**—Once you have a good rhythm and can move your sandwich in time with the machine, you need to choose the best combination of needle and thread. Needle and thread are important in making the perfect stitch. You need to ensure that the needle is fit for the fabric and will not cause damage. The thread also has to work well with the needle and bring out the beauty of the quilt. The good news is that you have a chance to try out as many needle-thread combinations as you wish, until you find exactly what you are looking for. Remember to write down the combinations as you try them on your practice sandwich.

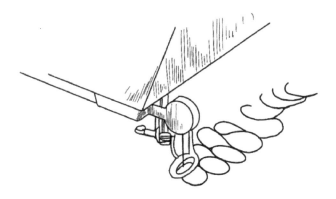

8. **Quilt**—When you find the right doodle and have the perfect needle and thread, it is time to quilt, though still on your practice sandwich. You should keep quilting the pattern, balancing the speed, and practicing until you get even stitches. However, do not be afraid to try out a real project once you think you're ready. In a

short while, you will look back at your first quilt with pride at how far you have come.

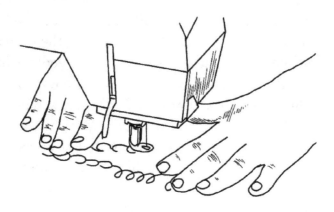

Practice

The only way to get perfect stitches and make beautiful, error-free patterns is through practice. You should make several practice sandwiches of different fabric and use them to figure out which ones work well with different patterns and threads. Do not tire from trying out different designs on your practice sandwiches; at the end of the day, you will be proud of the project you undertake. You will have an opportunity to create doodles that are unique to you, know your preferred needles, and understand which fabric pairs best with which thread.

Chapter Summary

The only sure way to get started is by doing and doodling. Do so, and you're on your way to becoming an expert free-motion quilter.

- Doodle away! You can start with cursive letters.

- Draw on paper before moving to stitching.

- Practice your name; charity begins at home.

- Mistakes are the pathways to greatness and perfection, so embrace them.

In the next chapter, you will have an opportunity to create and stitch your first design!

Chapter Ten:
Making Your First Design

Since you have been practicing your doodling and have a solid grasp on your foot-hand coordination, it is time to create your first design. Yes, you are now transitioning from a beginner to a quilter with a little experience. In this chapter, you will get the opportunity and guidance to create your first quilt design. We will start simple and easy to get your confidence levels up. As usual, here is a step-by-step guide on creating your first design.

What You Need:

- Threads

- Needle according to thread

- Quilt

Steps:

1. **Create Your Quilt Sandwich**—You may not be very enthusiastic about the taping down of the fabric and putting all those pins, but stay encouraged. This particular sandwich is for your first design. You can start with a small quilt sandwich that will not take a long time to baste. As you begin, working on smaller projects is helpful because they will be easier to

complete. Also, in case of mistakes, it is also faster to undo stitches from a small quilt than a large one. Once you are confident of your ability to design and quilt, you can gradually increase the size of your project.

2. **Prepare Your Machine**—Clean and oil your machine, prepare it as we discussed, and put in a new needle and thread, ready to quilt.

3. **Position Your Quilt**—You need your quilt to be right under the needle point where you want to start. Ideally, it is recommended to start quilting in the middle and move around to keep the sandwich from shifting. However, this is free-motion quilting, meaning you can begin from anywhere. The key determinant of where to start lies in your design and intended pattern.

4. **Start Quilting**—Lower the presser foot and begin quilting. How hard you drive the presser foot determines how fast your machine moves. You can either go slowly or fast—the choice is yours.

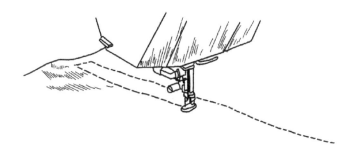

5. **Move the Quilt**—In free-motion quilting, you have to remember that you are in control. Move the quilt at a constant pace. You need to find a balanced rhythm between your hands and feet to avoid looping. You are now creating stitches on your quilt. These stitches put together make your design.

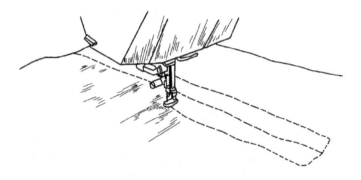

Let us look at some designs.

Simple Beginner Designs

a) Straight Lines

Some of the easiest stitches to do include making straight lines. If you are unsure of making your line straight, take a ruler and draw the line with a suitable marker. You can stitch along the line. Do not be overly concerned that your stitches are not even; your hand is the guide, and like everything human, there is no perfection. Strive for consistency while moving the quilt sandwich and keep in mind how hard you are pushing on the presser foot.

You can have straight lines on your borders or have them spit your quilt into two. You could have a series of straight or crisscrossing lines. Whatever you choose to do, it's all up to you, just keep your eye on the line and quilt away. There is always an element of elegance in simplicity. You may be amazed at the results.

b) Cursive Letters

In the previous chapter, we practiced cursive letters, and now is the time to apply them. The cursive L and C are particularly easy to apply and can be part of your designs. The cursive C may call for backing up on your line of stitching. Many beginners are scared of doing so, but you should not worry; there is nothing wrong with backing up on your stitches if you have to.

Cursive Es are also an easy beginner design to practice. You make them either straight up or upside down. From these, you can create loops, figure 8s, and some great border designs. You can also stitch them close together, meandering across the quilt to create a flowery pattern. Really, there is no limit to what simple cursive Es can achieve.

You can try writing your name on the quilt and even opt for your initials. Try quilting some letters on your sandwich. Free-motion quilting calls for using your imagination, do not limit yourself. Again, there is no hurry in free-motion stitching. Take as much as you need to get it right.

c) Loop da Loop

Meandering around the quilt is a good way to have fun and let your imagination run wild while still creating a beautiful design. Loops can also emulate cursive writing and are a good place to begin. Additionally, loops are great for filling an open background and just quilting around. Once you make a loop, you can stop where the threads cross and move to the opposite direction for the next loop. Having your loops opposite each other yet interconnected is a great way to create a random feel across the quilt. You can have big loops or small loops, or even mix them. Do what you please, as long as you are quilting.

As with all other designs, you can opt to draw them on the fabric to improve your confidence. Don't worry if you don't always land on the lines; they are there for general guidance and will wash off, leaving your stitches. Focus more on maintaining the speed of your hand in turn with that of your machine.

d) Flowers

You are probably thinking flowers are tough, and you're getting nervous. Relax—if you can loop, you can make a flower. Think of a simple flower; it is made of loops and a small circle in the middle. Now you can loop, which means you can conquer the flower. Make a loop for a petal and add a circle in the middle. The circle gives you a reference point of where to end your loop. Loop around, always going back to the circle, and you have a flower!

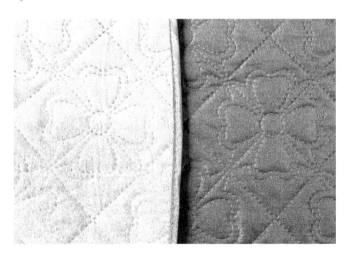

You can use a guide grip to help you make the loops and scallops, which are part of your flower.

Meander around, leaving a flower here and there, and soon, you will have a beautiful design.

e) Pebbles

Pebbles are merely circles and a classic filler design. Besides being simple to make, you can use them in different ways either by piling them together or scattering them across the quilt. However you chose to position your pebbles, they are a great design to incorporate. A tip to making the circles even, clean, and smooth is to look ahead. Your hands instinctively move toward your gaze. Look ahead, and your pebbles will be smooth. The size of the pebbles will depend entirely on you.

f) Switchbacks

You see that space between parallel lines? An ideal design for it is switchbacks. Switchbacks include designs that call for a back and forth movement, such as Us and Ns. They are also ideal for borders or sashing.

The key to making beautiful back and forths is to keep the lines about the same height, parallel, and straight as well as you can, with the curves nice and round. If need be, you can mark your quilt to help you trace the back and forth movement better.

g) Figure 8

Much like writing the eight, this design calls for stitching loops that resemble the number eight. Similar to switchbacks, you need to keep the top and bottom curved areas nice and round and relatively the same size.

Image source: Pinterest

h) Spirals

As the name suggests, this design involves making spiral lines on your quilt. The good news is that you can add your own flair. You can have rounded or pointed ones, depending on your preference and texture. You can also change the spacing between the lines. The most important thing to remember when stitching spirals is to allow yourself space to leave the inside of the spiral.

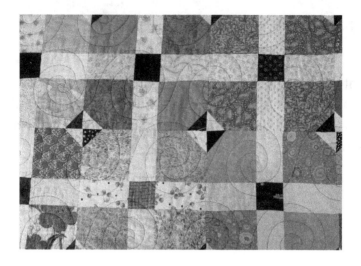

An advantage of this method is that it allows you to travel all over your quilt, and you can even echo the design. You may want to doodle the design first to get used to it before starting up your machine.

i) Star

You can also create a star design by moving the quilt in a star shape. You may want to pause slightly at the top to give your mind a chance to readjust in that direction and prevent it from making more of a curve than a sharp tip.

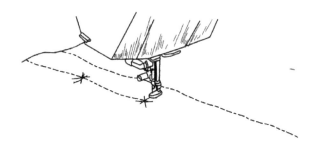

j) Stippling

Stippling is probably the most quilted design in the history of quilting, and for a good reason; it goes anywhere and adds texture very quickly. For ease of understanding, stippling is merely wiggly lines or meandering without ever crossing stitches. You can make your stitches sharp or round, depending on your preference. Yours may look different from the others.

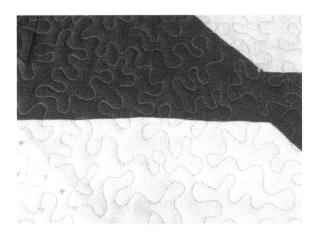

What you need to keep in mind is how to get out of tight areas and keep quilting. If you get to the edge, you can tie off your stitching and move on to another spot.

k) Pumpkins

Pumpkins are quite pretty, and they look just as beautiful on quilts. As a beginner, you can learn how to quilt pumpkins. They do not have to be perfect—after all, they come in all sizes and shapes. Once you have mastered the loop, you can do the pumpkin. The best way is to start from the top, traveling around to make the external shell, dropping down the middle and up again, before making a sort-of rectangle stem at the top. You can then get out by making vines, either via single loops or meanders to the next pumpkin. You need to keep in mind where to get out of your pumpkin and make the next one.

Consider drawing the design on a piece of paper and practicing, so you can have a good feel of it before you begin stitching.

l) Paisley

When creating a paisley design on your quilt, you would start with a teardrop shape and pivot and echo around the teardrop. As you echo, increase the distance between the curves, but decrease the distance as you go back to the starting point. This is the basic design. From there you can echo the teardrop as much as you want and branch out to start another teardrop, angling in a different direction. Repeat the process.

The examples given here are only a guide to get you started. However, there is no limit to what design you can choose for your quilt. Below is a suggestion of a quilting design for you to start with.

Sample Design

You can begin by combing a straight line and a star. From the left corner, stitch a straight line and set a particular distance to create a star by quickly moving the quilt into a star shape. The distance between stars will depend on the length of your quilt and your preference. You can repeat the pattern by stitching in uneven rows. Creating uneven rows helps disguise the rows of stitching on the quilt. The key here is to work systematically from one row to the next.

In the middle of the quilt, you can free-handedly write your name or any other text of your choice before proceeding with the line and star design. If you are nervous, you can mark the pattern and trace your name on the fabric. That way, you can have something to follow as a guide.

In no time, you will have created your very first design. Congratulations! You are on your way to becoming a celebrated quilter.

Chapter Summary

Developing and executing a design of your own is not rocket science. All the designs you see on quilts are products of people like you. Remember:

- There is no limit to what you can create.

- Start with simple designs; even straight lines, can make a beautiful design.

- Gradually take on more designs in scope and details.

- Always draw your design on paper to give your mind a chance to internalize it before transferring it to the quilt.

- Practice.

In the next chapter, we look at filler designs and how to use them to make your quilt more or less engaging.

Chapter Eleven:
Filler Designs

Choosing a Filler Design

Although it may seem easy, choosing a good filler design can turn into a tricky affair. You could choose a filler that will not blend well with your choice of a design and make your quilt look different from what you intended. In most cases, your choice of a filler design will be largely dependent on the kind of texture you want in your quilt. For example, you may choose to have a lot of movement in one particular area and none in another. You could also choose to have an even texture across the entire project.

The trick to selecting a great filler design for your quilt lies in the amount of contrast you prefer. If you want to showcase your main design and make it pop, then you will need a contrasting filler. On the other hand, you can choose a blending filler to hide the main design or make it subtle. Filler designs can also hide your imperfections, thus making your quilt a masterpiece, regardless of any mistakes. Keep in mind that the level of contrast is determined by the design shape, thread color, design direction, and filler's density.

Creating your Filler Design

You now know what a filler is and can now choose which type to use in which situation. You probably have a preference already. Now is the time to create a filler design of your own.

What You Need

- Threads.

- Fabric.

- Needle according to thread.

Steps

1. **Prepare Your Quilt Sandwich**—Choose what kind of quilt you want to create and go through the basting process. Even for smaller projects, you will have to ensure that your sandwich is done properly. Remember to keep it taut but not stretched. The choice of how big a quilt you should make is solely yours. As a suggestion, beginners should use a smaller quilt, just to see a finished product and keep them encouraged. Even going through the basting process for a small project will give you experience and help you improve.

2. **Prepare Your Machine**—If you have been using the machine, clean it to get rid of any lint, then oil it. You want your machine running

smoothly and without much inhibitions. Put your thread and needle in and ensure you opt for the needle down setting. That way, you can move your fabric in the direction you want while it is well-anchored by the needle.

3. **Position the Sandwich Under the Needle**—You want your starting point to be sitting right on the needle, so when you press down on the presser foot, all you would have to do is move the fabric and get quilting. It is recommendable that you have a general idea of your design, so you can know where to start from and in which direction to follow.

4. **Quilt a Boundary**—You need to quilt the boundary so you can have a marked beginning and end to work with. You can do simple double lines and make a pattern in between the lines, like pebbles or even swirls.

5. **Quilt Your Design Freehand**—With clearly marked boundaries, it is now time to quilt. You can quilt your design of choice freehand.

6. **Use Fillers**—Most often, there will only be so
    much of the design you can quilt. For example,
    if you choose to quilt huts, you will have spaces
    between them. That is where the fillers come
    in. As another example, you could stitch a
    name at the center of the quilt, though such a
    design leaves the quilt looking empty. Filler
    designs are meant to fill the open parts of the
    quilt and draw attention to the central design.
    Meanders, pebbles, stipples, snowflakes, and
    loops are all great fillers. Once you have the
    hang of them, you can stitch all over the quilt
    without any problems.

    You can make smaller versions of your central
    designs be fillers. For example, if you are

stitching spiralling circles, you can make small pebbles or spirals across the quilt.

7. **Secure Your Design**—You certainly do not want to have your stitches running, not after all the hard work you put in. Therefore, you need to secure your stitches as you start and end. Simply make two stitches and go back on them to ensure they do not run. In most cases, the repetition will be hardly visible.

Some Common Filler Designs

Stippling—As the ultimate quilting design, stippling has been and continues to be one of the most used filler designs. We all love stippling so much because it provides texture and interest. Besides, as an independent filler, stippling goes anywhere on the quilt and can even form the background for a pattern. For beginners, this is important to learn. You can start by practicing drawing on a piece of paper before moving to stitching.

Clamshells—They really are semi-circles stacked in rows that fill up the open areas on the quilt beautifully. Since you can stack them, you can also use them in tight areas.

Parallel lines—You can stitch parallel lines across your quilt as a filler. The interesting bit is that they do not have to be straight; you could make them wavy or curved, or even uneven.

Pebbles—Pebbles add texture and draw interest in a quilt. You would start by stitching a simple circle, then add another next to it. Keep adding until you cover the space you need. You can vary the size.

Mixing and Matching Your Design

You are not restricted to one filler per quilt; you can have as many as you please and either spread them across the quilt or vary them per each block. You can use, for example, pebbles, nested spirals, and lines to make a rich texture. Create your own unique design and personalize each quilt. Free-motion quilting starts with "free," so feel free to make each quilt your own.

Chapter Summary

Filler designs can either make your main design to pop or take attention away from it. From the chapter, we learned that:

- There are many types of filler designs, including independent stippling, pivotal, stacked, central, echo, and edge-to-edge.

- Your choice of filler will depend on your intended overall look and the spaces you are working with. Some fillers won't work for small and tight spaces.

- You are not restricted to any one filler; you can mix some together.

You are now a quilter if you have implemented what we have learned so far. All you have to do is keep practicing, and you should be a pro in no time. To keep the practice up, in the next chapter, we will make a Christmas gift. You can make as many as you want for friends and relatives.

Chapter Twelve:
How to Make Sashes and Borders

Sashes

Sashes are strips of fabric that frame the quilt block, making it easy to distinguish your blocks, or make them pop. The block could be a single piece or several. Ideally, sashing is between 2½ inches to 3½ inches wide.

Here is a simple guide on how to make sashes for your quilt.

1. **Lay Out Your Blocks in the Preferred Order**—Take the first block and put strips on each side, then pin.

2. **Stitch**—The seam allowance should be about ¼ inch. When in doubt of where to stitch, always do ¼ inch. Make your stitches as even as possible.

3. **Press**—After stitching, take your iron box and press the opposite side first before turning your fabric, while also pressing the top part. Once you press, the seams should go out toward the sashing.

4. **Second and Subsequent Blocks**—Take the second block and stitch ¼ inch, press the

opposite side, then the top side, ensuring that the seams go toward the sashing. Repeat the process for all the blocks.

5. **The Edges**—When you get to the edge, add another piece of sashing. Remember that you will have borders to work on.

6. **Join the Rows**—Once done, measure the length of the quilt and add some inches, about 2½ inches. Stitch the sashing, then join to the subsequent row. Ensure the seam comes in towards the sashing, leaving your blocks with no bumps.

7. **Trim Off Excess**—Take a ruler and measure excess fabric to remove. Your top fabric is now ready for basting.

Borders

Your quilt isn't quite complete without borders. Borders on a quilt help bring out its center and give it a sense of wholeness. When it comes to borders, you have many options—you can have a simple strip or make them intricately pieced. Alternatively, you can simply have a straight border.

As a beginner, you may want to keep your borders simple. Here are some options:

- **Strips**—You can add strips of a single fabric around the sides of the quilt. Make border strips in pairs and add them to opposite edges.

- **Straight Borders**—In many cases, the sides of a quilt will differ in length because of stretching during quilting. To maintain a good shape and look, many quilters opt to measure the length and width of the quilt from its top to the bottom through the midpoint, so they can get the appropriate measurements. From then, it is easy to sew borders to the two longest sides before moving to the shortest sides.

Other quilters decide to measure the quilt at multiple points, then get the average of them and consider that to be the running length.

Quilting the First Two Borders

Here is a simple guide on how to sew the initial two borders on your quilt.

1. **Find the Midpoint**—You can achieve this by folding one of the borders crosswise in half to find its midpoint and crease it a little at that spot. You also need to find the horizontal midpoint of the quilt.

2. **Carefully Place the Border**—You should have your border placed along the quilt's side. Be careful to ensure that the right sides are together with matching midpoints. You can pin the border to the quilt to prevent it from shifting.

3. **Match the Bottom Border to the Bottom Edge**—As you did with the top, ensure that your bottom border matches the quilt's edge and pin them together. You may have to ensure that you pin at close intervals to ensure the lengths match well and raw edges are well-aligned on the entire side of the quilt.

4. **Sew the Borders**—You can use a seam allowance of ¼ inches. Remember to remove the pins as you get close to them to prevent them from bending and needles from breaking.

5. **Press**—After stitching, press the seam allowance toward the border.

6. **Replicate**—Use the same method to do the remaining opposite sides of the borders.

Chapter Summary

In this chapter, we learned how to do sashes and borders. Here are some key points from the chapter:

- Sashes and borders help to accentuate your central design.

- When using blocks, always keep your sashes and borders within the same size of the block.

- Always press the seam allowance toward the border.

- Don't leave your sashes and borders plain; quilt some designs.

Now that you can quilt and tie up the project with beautiful borders, let's try a Christmas special.

Chapter Thirteen:
Free-Motion Quilting Christmas Special

What You Need:

1. Red fabric for the external layer.

2. White fabric for the bedding.

3. White threads.

Steps:

1. **Prepare Your Quilt Sandwich—**By now, you are probably already an expert at basting. Through practice, you have mastered the art of making your fabric taught without stretching it and choosing the right batting for your sandwich. Here is another opportunity to perfect your skills.

2. **Now Prepare Your Quilting Machine—** Clean and oil your machine, install your darning foot, and lower your feed dogs. Set the stitch length to zero. You are now the boss— and you deserve it.

3. **Prepare Your Holly Design—**Christmas is the season to celebrate and spread some love and cheer. The holly design includes berries

and spiky leaves. The best thing to do is draw the design on a piece of paper first, so you can practice a bit beforehand. Drawing on paper first will help you internalize the design. You also get an opportunity to visualize how your final project will look.

4. **Slowly Start Quilting the Design on Your Quilt Sandwich**—Quilting a holly design is much like stitching the pebbles and the star. You have had practice and are ready to make the best holly design you have ever made. You can be confident that this will be your best project yet. Slowly start by meandering before stitching the berries. Once done, you can stitch the spiky leaf. The secret to achieving those sharp spikes lies in slowing down, so you can have time to focus and begin the curved part of the leaf. The spikes are similar to the stars; you can enjoy the fruits of time spent practicing.

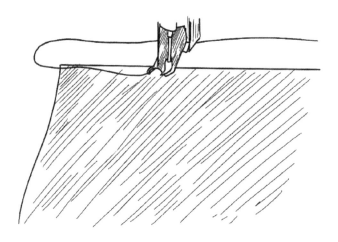

5. **Remember Not to Sew Twice in the Middle of Your Design**—Although you may be tempted to sew twice, resist the urge and keep your design clean and elegant. It will also help to keep your fabric undamaged.

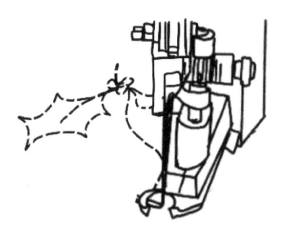

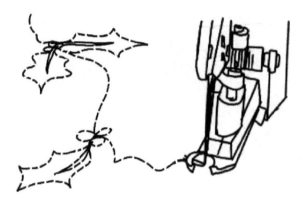

6. **Use Fillers**—If you find that you have made some small mistakes in your design, you can add some fillers. You can use them to hide any unbalanced areas and keep the focus off any part of the quilt you do not want to draw attention to.

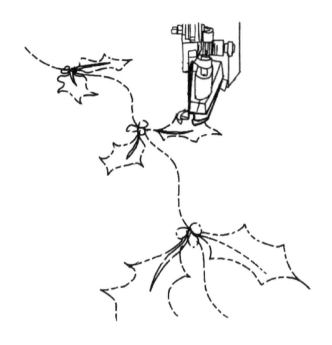

7. **Secure It by Double-Stitching the Last Two Stitches**—You do not want that beautiful holly design to start running before you even get an opportunity to show it off. To keep everything secure, double-stitch the last two stitches to keep them well-anchored.

8. **Gift Away**—This quilt can be the perfect gift for any loved one. You could even stitch your name and the names of those you want to give to on the quilt, making it more personalized. Gifting quilts will also give you an opportunity to show off what you have achieved so far.

9. **Appreciate the Feedback**—Quilters are a self-conscious group, and often, their own

worst critics. Enjoy and appreciate the compliments. You need to realize that those around you genuinely appreciate the hard work you put into the quilt and likely won't notice minor mistakes. If they do, it's the last of their concern. Take in the compliments and let them motivate you to take up bigger projects. You could even get orders and start making money.

Table Runner Project

Now that you have given others something for Christmas, how about something for yourself—or if you are a giver, for someone else. You can use this project to hone your skills and gain some experience. Practice makes perfect, and what better way to keep practicing than through interesting projects. This time, let's try making a table runner.

What You Need:

1. Quilt fabric.

2. Cotton batting.

3. Cotton thread, 100%.

4. Safety pins.

5. Sewing needles.

6. Monofilament thread (optional).

7. Masking tape.

Steps

1. **Bast the Sandwich**—By now, you are getting the hang of basting, but a quick reminder never hurts. Take your fabric and lay it out on a clean and flat surface, then tape the back to the surface. Remember that the key is to have it taut but not stretched. Place your batting on top of the fabric, but do not tape it. You would then put the top fabric on the batting and smoothen the sandwich. You can now begin placing your pins one or two inches apart.

   An important tip is to pin away from seam allowances and allow for seams to be quilted in the ditch or along a design line. You do not want your walking foot to catch on the safety pins. Also, not having to remove safety pins along the way will save you a lot of time.

2. **Set Up the Sewing Machine**—Install your quilting foot, thread the machine, and set the needle down function. Having the needle down is like giving you an extra hand, and help is welcome. Also, adjust your tension setting. You are now ready for the actual work.

3. **Ditch Quilting**—Remember that this is sewing on the lower side of a seam and as close as possible. You have to manoeuvre the sandwich. With ditch quilting, you have to be keen on seeing where the needle pierces through the fabric. Since the stitches are close

to the edge without hitting it and stitch lines are straight, your work is to keep the eye on the needle. Again, remember to sew at your speed. You should not take ditch quilting as a race— what you need is control. Use whatever speed that allows you to feel in control.

4. **Stabilize the Quilt**—A way to stabilize your quilt is by quilting the line that lies closest to the quilt's center, running North and South. Next, quilt the ditch that is either the centermost or running East and West. Since it's a table runner, you may find that some of the lines are borders.

5. **Fill in the Ditch**—Fill in with the ditch quilting, working out to the edge from the central lines. You can then flip your sandwich at 180 degrees and start again from the center.

6. **Quilt Around the Outside Edge**—You need to make a stitching line around the edge, outside of the sandwich. Keep it at less than ¼ inches, so you ensure it's within the seam allowance. The binding will cover this later.

7. **Use Fillers**—Free-motion quilting and ditch quilting use different eye positions, and you are better off finishing with ditch quilting before starting free-motion. You do not have to switch back and forth. I suggest doing filler designs last because they tend to draw up the quilt.

Choose a filler design—stippling is a good bet—but do not limit yourself.

8. **Distribute Your Quilting**—Your table runner may be a bit long, depending on your table, but ensure that you quilt as evenly as you can over it. Remember that quilted areas tend to draw up heavily.

Chapter Summary

You should now have confidence in your ever-improving free-motion quilting skills and can produce basic designs. Gifting quilts that you made by yourself is a major milestone and needs a celebration! I am certain that you now have a good understanding of your machine and have created a rapport with it by now.

From here, the sky's the limit. Keep practicing, keep quilting, and keep finishing those projects, no matter how bad you may think they are.

Inspiring Gallery of Finished Quilts

Final Words

The hardest part of any journey is the beginning, and they say, "The journey of a thousand miles starts with a single step." You have come so far already, and if you are here, you deserve a pat on the back.

Throughout this journey, you have gained a wealth of knowledge on free-motion quilting. You now have a better understanding of your machine and what you need to make your quilting experience enjoyable. You can choose your thread and pair it with an appropriate needle, in addition to setting up your machine for quilting. Your basting skills have grown considerably with practice, and you can certainly begin a project. You can make, mark, stitch, and complete any of your designs. From now on, gifting will be easier because, no matter the season, you can quilt something personal for someone.

Quilting is not just any other activity. Quilting is a way of life and antidote from life's stresses and sicknesses; it is a place of peace and enjoyment. Mastering free-motion quilting is a goal that gives much joy, as long as you are willing to put in the effort. Allocate time each day. Fifteen or twenty minutes each day will have you creating masterpieces soon enough. Like all important things in life, you have to commit.

Above all, enjoy the process, appreciate every stitch, and celebrate any finished project—no matter how small. As you quilt freely and grow continually, may your bobbin never run out of thread!

CPSIA information can be obtained
at www.ICGtesting.com
Printed in the USA
LVHW031318151222
735289LV00010B/2259

9 781951 035815